Words On A Page

Monologues for Young Performers

Regina Moore

&

Cali Elizabeth Moore

moore
Entertainment
Publishing

Published by Moore Entertainment Publishing, LLC.
417 Welshwood Drive, Suite 109
Nashville, TN 37211
(615) 831-0039
MooreEntertainment.com

Words On A Page: Monologues for Young Performers

ISBN-13: 978-0-9842909-0-1 / ISBN-10: 0-9842909-0-7
Library of Congress Control Number: 2009910821

Cover design by Audra Harvey
Interior design by Lea Collins
Project managed by abrasiveInk.

PRINTED IN THE UNITED STATES OF AMERICA

"Finally: a monologue book with quality, interesting,
and age-appropriate material!
Regina has applied her years of auditioning experience
as a top Casting Director and
Cali hers as both an actress and child acting coach;
together they have written a wide selection of monologues
with instructions on how to choose one that works for you.
This book is a *must* for your library of acting material!"

Joy Pervis

Talent Agent, J Pervis Talent Agency; National Talent Scout, Osbrink Agency
Joy is recognized for discovering, developing, and/or representing young actors,
including: Dakota Fanning, Lucas Till, Raven Symone, Kyle Massey, and Elijah Kelley.

CONTENTS

Part 2: Boys

Part 3: Girls

Part 4: Young Women & Young Men

About the Authors

Words on a Page: Monologues for Young Performers

INTRODUCTION

You've seen it a million times. You go to an audition and some-one performs a monologue that is outdated, inappropriate, or so cheesy that it's not relatable. If you've ever found yourself asking, "Where are all the good monologues?" you're not alone. That's what we said! After searching and coming up empty handed, we began writing our own monologues. Years later, at the request of many desperate parents and frustrated talent agents, we compiled some of our favorites in *Words on a Page.*

Words on a Page is for the serious child actor looking to "wow" their audience with relatable, current, and interesting monologues. Whether you are five years old or eighteen years old, there are monologues in this book that will help you grow as an actor and develop your performance. *Words on a Page* features monologues of different lengths and subject matter with both male and female focus. Each one has been thoroughly tested by young actors and used for every type of audition, from theatre to film.

Every aspect of this book is designed to be easy to use. Each section includes a wide range of monologues as well as tips for honing your skill. Take the time to read through every monologue in the section before making your selection to be sure you choose the perfect fit. Longer monologues are laid out on facing pages to minimize page turning and make them easier to copy. Each line ends on a full word to help you find your place more easily. Monologues for younger children are in a larger font with more generous spacing to make the material easier to read. Subtle emphasis and directions are marked to help you bring each monologue to life, but we've left plenty of room for you to visualize each scenario and develop the personality of each character.

We encourage you to make these monologues *more* than just words on a page. You are an actor. Show them what you can do! Inside this book are the materials to help you do it.

Regina Moore &
Cali Elizabeth Moore

PART 1
Very Young Actors

This section is designed for the very young child actor. At this stage, industry professionals are looking for the ability to talk about a subject with clarity and confidence. This means it is important to choose a monologue that is engaging and comfortable for each child, ideally with a subject to which they seem drawn. It will show in their delivery.

While age is a factor, the appropriateness of a monologue can't be determined specifically by the age but rather by the child's ability to memorize, recall, and deliver it well. Some children will need a short monologue because their ability to read takes precedence over a longer, more in-depth piece of work. Some children, though they may not read well or even at all, have strong memorization skills and may be able to master a larger monologue. Be sensitive to the strengths and abilities of each individual child when making your choice.

SCARY STORIES

Cali Elizabeth Moore

I am so shocked! Today in class the teacher read us a story called "Goldilocks and the Three Bears."

In the story, a little girl named Goldilocks breaks into a house. She takes their food, breaks their chairs, and sleeps in their beds! This girl is nuts! People didn't live in this house. BEARS did! Bears . . . with sharp teeth that eat little girls.

Then she escapes with her life. I was not prepared for such a frightening story! I almost cried. I think scary stories should not be read to kids at school.

I just hope I can sleep tonight.

EMERGENCY
Cali Elizabeth Moore

(ON THE PHONE)

Hello? Is this 911? My mom fell on the floor and she isn't getting up. I tried to talk to her but she looks asleep. My dad is at work. They told me at school that if there is an emergency I should call 911. Will you come and help my mom?

New Kid

Regina Moore

I am a little nervous. Today is the first day at a new school. I don't know anyone and no one knows me. I hope my teacher is nice and likes new kids. My last teacher liked new kids.

Well, I guess I'll go in. Wish me luck!

Veterinarian

Cali Elizabeth Moore

I love animals. Every kind of animal! I have a dog named Swift. I named him Swift because he is really fast. I also have a fish named Bubbles. Bubbles is a really good swimmer. My dad says I should be a veterinarian. He says veterinarians are animal doctors. I think that would be pretty cool. So when I grow up, you can just call me Animal Doctor *(YOUR NAME)*.

My Cool Sister

Cali Elizabeth Moore

My sister is the coolest person I know! She always looks so pretty and she always has her nails painted. She never lets me in her room, but one time I snuck in there. She has magazines and makeup everywhere. It was so cool. I hope I grow up to be just like her!

TRADING DAD

Regina Moore

I ask mom, "Where is Dad?" She always says, "Your dad is at work." When she says it, she sounds kind of mad.

When Mom gets mad and tells Dad to stay home, he says, "I can't give you all of the things you need unless I work." Mom just cries and says that she'd rather live in a little house and take the new car back.

I think she just wants Dad to be around more so we can be happy.

So do I.

THE BEACH

Cali Elizabeth Moore

My family goes to the beach every summer. It is my favorite thing to do all summer long. I love to swim in the ocean. I like the waves and the sand. Sometimes I even see a fish or a crab. I always pick up shells by the shore with my dad, too. The beach is my favorite place to go in the summer!

Dance Class

Cali Elizabeth Moore

Yesterday my mom took me to my first dance class. It was so much fun! I got to twirl and tumble. I got to shimmy and shake. I can't wait till next week! Dance class is my new favorite thing! *(TWIRLS)* Look at me!

KINDERGARTEN

Regina Moore

My teacher, Ms. Bledsoe, told me she wants me to speak at the Kindergarten graduation. I am very excited, but I am not sure what I am supposed to say. I could talk about the first day of school, or our first field trip. Maybe she wants me to talk about learning. Well, whatever I say, I hope she likes it. She is my favorite teacher so far!

PRINCESS

Cali Elizabeth Moore

In a few years, I know that my parents are going to tell me the truth. I am a princess. I have known it for years. When my mom calls me special, it is because I am a princess. So until they tell me, I'll pretend to be "normal." That could be very difficult.

SCARED

Cali Elizabeth Moore

I get scared sometimes. Not always. I'm not a baby or anything. It's just that sometimes when I'm alone in my room, it's scary.

I know there's no one there, but in the dark I can't be sure. Sometimes I pull the covers over my head and close my eyes really tight. I don't do this all the time; only when I get spooked.

Usually, I get scared when there is a storm, or I hear the floor creaking in the hall. When the wind hits the branch outside my bedroom window, it taps my window. That makes me nervous. It's the wind, of course, but what if . . . it's . . . a GHOST! I know ghosts and that stuff aren't real, but what if they are?

One night my mom hired a babysitter who didn't make me go to sleep. She hasn't been back. I stayed up with her and watched a scary movie with ghosts in it. I know this sounds crazy, but they looked pretty real.

The movie was in a scary house . . . like mine. With a normal family . . . like mine. Then the ghosts came in and got them! Is that what is next for me?

Look, I told you I am not a baby, but these are the facts. Wouldn't *you* be scared?

FOUR CATS
Regina Moore

I have four cats at home. One likes to play with a mouse. Sugar would rather play with my striped fish, if I would let her. Prince likes to play with string, and Lucky just likes to sleep in front of the door. Sometimes they all curl up together. I love my cats because I always have someone to play with.

FISHING

Regina Moore

Dad wants to take me fishing! I am a girl. My mom calls me her little angel. Tell me: when was the last time *you* saw an angel holding a fishing pole?

Fish stink, they're slimy, and what if I get wet? No, no, no, Dad, I hate to break it to you, but *this* little angel will get wet only in a swimming pool and eat fish only if you buy it in a restaurant. I know we need some father and daughter time, but fishing is *not* the answer.

MEAN SISTER
Cali Elizabeth Moore

My sister always gets me in trouble. Like last week, she ate all the cookies and blamed me. Or today: she hid mom's keys and said I knew where they were. I don't know what do! It's just not fair! I wish my sister wasn't so mean.

CHEF DAD
Cali Elizabeth Moore

My dad is the best cook in the whole world! Everything he cooks is so good!

He makes fried chicken, macaroni and cheese, and even spaghetti. My favorite is fish tacos. MMMM! Sometimes he lets me help, too. One day, I'll be a good cook just like my dad.

THE LIST

Cali Elizabeth Moore

I have decided that every parent gets a list: a list passed down from generation to generation of parents. This list contains things to nag their kids about.

I am positive that every parent has a copy. How else do you explain different kids' parents nagging about the same things? Like last Tuesday; I was at John's house and his mother told him to clean his room because it looked "like a pig sty." Then when I got home, guess what my mother told me? "Clean your room; it looks like a pig sty." The same exact words!

I talked to a few of my other friends at school. They said that their moms' say a lot of the same things *my* mom says. Things like, "No dessert until you clean your plate," or "Because I said so," or "Give your sister a hug and tell her you're sorry."

So I am here today to let all of you parents know: I'm spreading the word about the list. We may be kids, but we're on to your little game. And we don't like it!

SCHOOL ISN'T EASY

Regina Moore

My dad always comes home from work and says that he is tired. I know he goes to work every day and sometimes he has to work on Saturday, but what if he had to go to school?

School isn't easy. Parents do not understand the pressure we have to deal with. Homework every day, friends not always being your friend, and teachers either like you or make your life a nightmare. School is work, too.

I can't wait to grow up and go to work. It sounds like a piece of cake!

POLICEMAN

Regina Moore

I want to be a policeman, when I grow up. They drive fast and chase people in cars with sirens. If anyone else does that, they get in trouble and go to jail, but not policemen. A policeman gets to talk on the T.V. and tell people what happened and get awards for being brave.

Yeah, I want to be a policeman. It can't be *that* hard.

MISSING CARRIE

Regina Moore

Carrie is moving away and I am going to miss her. She lives next door to me and we do *everything* together. I wonder if she will find a friend that likes her as much as me? I think it will be hard so I hope she finds a really good friend as soon as she gets there.

Oh, me? I make friends easy. I will meet somebody, and if I am lucky, maybe another girl will move in next door.

(*SHE REALIZES*) What if it's not a girl? What if a boy moves in right next to me?

No. I am not even going to think about it. I am not ready for *that!*

PET STORE

Regina Moore

Mom took me to a pet store today. I saw the cutest puppies, some big ones, some little ones, and some in between. I saw some birds, too. There were all different colors and sizes.

Mom and I picked out some fish to take home, and we bought a special tank for them to live in. She said that we're going to put the tank in the livingroom because that way we can all enjoy them.

We also saw some spiders and lizards. Mom did not want to take them home. She said they could get loose. I think we were pretty safe deciding on the fish. At least when we put them in the tank, we know they're not going anywhere!

THE HOSPITAL

Regina Moore

I've never been to the hospital until last night. I fell off the top bunk and the doctor said I broke my leg. We waited in the waiting room for a long time and then my leg really started to hurt. I started to scream.

Then the nurses came and got me. They took me through these big doors where there were machines and everything was beeping. It hurt a whole lot, but I didn't cry. They put a cast on my leg and some nurses signed it.

I think I like the hospital. But next time I go back, I hope I'm just visiting!

SANTA
Regina Moore

It's almost Christmas time and *that* means Santa. I hope he comes to see me. Mom said that Santa doesn't like it if you wait up for him. But I want to see him! I gave him a really long Christmas list. I wonder if he can fit it all down the chimney?

Oh! I better go. I think I hear him coming.

Coming Home

Regina Moore

I was watching TV the other night and I saw a show about this kid being kidnapped by his own parents. The show was talking about a boy who was stuck between a mother and father. They were fighting over who he would live with. The father took the kid and the mother didn't know where they went. That is hard on everybody. The mom doesn't know where her son is and the dad is taking a big chance just leaving like that. They said he could go to jail.

I feel sorry for the mom and dad, but I feel sorry for the kid most of all. The boy didn't ask for any of those problems. Can you image how that must make him feel? Your mom and dad are the two most important people in your life; they are the ones that you trust.

Even though they are fighting over him, I hope he knows the problem is something else. Something his parents are trying to deal with, not him. He isn't the cause of any of it.

I hope his father realizes that if he really loves his son, he will just take him back and work out whatever problems they have. If they both loved him, they wouldn't put him in the middle like that.

In Love
Cali Elizabeth Moore

Why can't *I* be in love? Just because I'm in elementary school doesn't mean I don't know what love is! No one understands.

I am in love with Paul. He's a boy in my class. We pass notes to each other and talk on the phone every night. We even sit next to each other at lunch.

Sometimes I'll catch him writing "Lauren and Paul Forever" on his homework. He writes it in the corner really small so no one can see it. But I do!

I told my mom about it and told her we were in love and she laughed. She LAUGHED! Like I had told a joke or something. She said I "think" I'm in love with everyone at this age because I'm boy crazy.

Boy crazy? I am only crazy for one boy: Paul. So does that make it some "childish crush," as my sister puts it? I don't think so. I am in love. IN LOVE, I tell you! And I'm going to shout it from the intercom at school! So there!

DENTIST

Cali Elizabeth Moore

My mom says I have to go to the dentist. She says he will clean my teeth with a special toothbrush to make my teeth sparkle. At first I was scared. But then my big sister said it was kind of fun. So maybe this dentist won't be so bad!

PART 2
Girls

This section focuses on things girls experience at home and in school: boyfriends, family issues, the loss of a friend, and the new surprises in life that they need to process and vocalize. There are monologues describing pain, frustration, growth, happiness, and humor.

It is important to look through this selection of monologues and read each one, making sure you understand what the character is thinking and feeling so you can deliver it convincingly—as if you just had the same experience. Finding a good monologue is like finding a good pair of jeans: it has to fit just right or people will think you borrowed it. Everyone will know that it does not belong to you. It has to be the perfect fit.

ANYTHING CAN HAPPEN

Cali Elizabeth Moore

I've always loved this ring.

When I was little, my mother wore it on special occasions. She loved it so much. She kept it in a beautiful blue and red glass box when she wasn't wearing it.

When she was cooking dinner or putting on her makeup, I would sneak into her room and peek into the box. I'd just look at it. I wouldn't even touch it. It was just so beautiful. It seemed like it was magic or something.

Mom would always tell me the story about how she got the ring. My grandpa took her to a dress store on her 9TH birthday and told her she could have anything she wanted. She saw a lady with bright pink lipstick looking at a dress with this ring on. She said she wanted that for her birthday. Grandpa said that wasn't for sale and it was out of his price range. The lady with the bright pink lipstick overheard their conversation, turned around, took the ring off, and gave it to my mom. Mom said it was proof that anything can happen.

She'd say that every day, it seemed like. "Don't give up; anything can happen." And then she'd flash the ring as the sparkling evidence.

Three months ago, mom gave me the ring. She got cancer. She wanted me to wear it and remember that anything can happen.

I tried. I prayed and I believed that she wasn't going to die. Not my mom. That just couldn't happen.

I found out anything could happen. Mom died a month after being diagnosed.

It was . . . it *is* . . . hard. Days seem so long. Problems seem so big. Sometimes I just want to sleep all day long. It just feels like I'll never have a good day again.

Then I look down and see this ring. I remember I'll see mom again and things will get better.

Anything can happen.

BEING PERFECT

Regina Moore

It seems like everyone thinks that they have to be perfect.

All of my friends at school think they have to have a perfect body, perfect clothes, and the perfect car. It's tough in high school balancing sports, school activities, and getting a job after school. Trying to maintain straight A's so I have a chance to go to a good college, get into a good school; it's hard.

Oh, and dating . . . I can't leave that part out. Dating the right guy and having the right friends that can get you into the right parties, and being nominated for Prom or Homecoming court. All of it . . . it can make or break your high school experience.

Lately, though, I've realized that I don't want to be like the other girls. Runway models with sucked in cheeks prancing around, pretending to be so together, but totally falling apart. They worry about what everyone thinks and make that their whole world.

When I graduate, this is just going to be a memory.

Some good, some bad, but it is not going to define who I am.

Last night when I was doing my homework after getting home from work and volleyball practice, I looked up the word "perfect." This is what it said: "Perfect—lacking in no respect; complete; in a state of complete excellence; without blemish or defect; faultless."

We all want to be the best we can be. But if we are afraid of living, then, to be perfectly honest, I don't *want* to be perfect.

SMARTEST KID IN CLASS

Cali Elizabeth Moore

I can't stand being the smartest kid in class! Everyone is always trying to copy off of my paper or ask me what I got on the test. LEAVE ME ALONE! Can't I be intelligent in peace?

Every kid in my class tries to be my partner for projects because they know I'll do a good job. And, of course, I have to do all the work. They are so lazy! And half the time they don't even understand what the project is about!

Mrs. Vickers always asks me to help her grade papers and run the attendance sheet to the office because she knows I can handle it. But every time she does, there is always some kid in class that makes a comment. You know, one of those "Aww, teacher's pet" comments.

I just ignore them, though. I get my revenge when we get our report cards, when the kids in class moan and cry about their grades. They say, "My parents are going to be so mad!" All the kids are so worried. Then the fun part comes when they ask me what I got on my report card. I just smile and say, "Straight A's."

Hey; maybe being the smartest kid in class isn't so bad, after all! Besides, they'll all be working for me one day, anyway!

Young Love

Cali Elizabeth Moore

I guess every little girl dreams of getting married. The perfect wedding. The perfect man. But my best friend Megan has got it all wrong.

She wants to get married—wait; no, I mean, she *is* getting married, in two weeks. She is marrying her boyfriend Logan.

Did I mention we are still in high school? Yeah; we are seventeen. So what is she *thinking*?

Almost worse, what are all my *friends* thinking? They keep telling Megan how excited they are for her and how beautiful she will look in her wedding dress. Hold on, everyone! Time out! Megan works at a fast food restaurant after school on Tuesdays and Thursdays. And Logan doesn't have a job at all because he has track practice after school. So how are you guys going to support yourselves? Where are you going to live? Has no one thought about this but me?

This is a huge mistake. *Huge.* Megan and Logan have only been dating for a year. I realize in high school time that is forever. But it's really not that long. People change. And what if they change in the next few years and find out they don't like each other? They won't just have to break up. They'll have to get a divorce.

Even if they do live happily ever after, they are missing out on all the fun stuff of high school. It's like cramming two huge life experiences into one tiny little time slot. All the memories and fun of high school—and, oh yeah, add planning and having a wedding in there, too. Don't they want to experience Prom as a young high school couple instead of married people? How weird is that?

I guess I never thought about all this before: what marriage means, what the high school experience really means. I just feel sad for Megan. And I guess, in a way, I feel happy for me. Is that bad? I just feel like for the first time I understand how important my high school experience is. And I'm just glad I'm not wasting it.

THE REMOTE

Regina Moore

Mom, Connor won't give me the remote. He watched the last three shows he wanted and it's my turn. My favorite show is next, Mom. I *have* to see it. Amber is suppose to find out if Lucas really loves her. This is not fair!

When will I get my own TV? It just makes sense that I have my own. That way I won't have to wait until it's my turn to see my shows.

(*PAUSE*) Oh, no; Dad's home. I can forget about seeing anything for the rest of the night. We will have to watch the news, the weather for tomorrow, and anything involving guns and horses. I guess I will never know if Amber finds her true love.

Women have no rights. We are held prisoner by the men in our lives. One day I will move away and buy my own TV and watch whatever I want. If my husband ever asks for the remote, he had better be ready to fight me for it. Now I know why Dad never asks for the remote when Mom is watching TV. At least I have *that* to look forward to.

TOMBOY

Regina Moore

I like to play basketball, football, soccer, tennis, volleyball, and run track. They say I'm an athlete, but my brother calls me a tomboy. I can't help it if I beat him every time we play a game.

My brother, Tommy, is two years older than me and is a pretty good athlete. He is probably better than me, but I know how to get under his skin. I know what to say to get his focus on me instead of what he's doing. I think *that* is why I beat him.

I also win every time I play against any of his friends. They hate it when I win. Their basketball coach, Mr. Robinson, asked me to come in during their practice and play one on one with the guys. Tommy gets really mad when I play him. I think it makes them try harder; that might be why the coach asks me to play against them.

I try not to beat him in front of his friends. Well, he *is* my brother. I have to give him a break. You know how boys are about losing to a girl. Mom says that Dad is the same way. I guess that's just the way things are.

HAPPY

Cali Elizabeth Moore

Sometimes I just get mad. I don't know why; I just do. I get all upset over nothing. It can be the tiniest little thing and I go nuts.

I've been known to scream, yell, argue, fight, cry, and anything else you can think of. I just can't help it. It's like I go into a trance or something. Like in those scary alien movies where the people don't know what they are doing because the aliens are controlling their mind.

(LAUGH) It used to be funny. You know, the nicknames: "hot headed Hannah." Mom would say, "Here she goes! She's about to explode! Look out!" And she'd always start laughing.

It's just that, well, now I'm too old to act like this. I'm too old to throw these fits. I'm losing friends and my grades are suffering and I feel like I'm losing my mind. I don't know what to do anymore. It's so embarrassing.

My teacher told me I should see the guidance counselor once a week. She said it would help me sort through everything in my head.

So every Tuesday at 11:30, I dart to the guidance office and hope no one will see me and think I am crazy. I mean, no one goes to the guidance office but the kids who have been to juvenile or the girls that are pregnant or the kids whose parents beat them. I don't want to be any of those!

The guidance counselor is really nice, though. Once I get inside, it's easy to relax. She talks to me about all kinds of stuff. I thought it would be . . . I don't know. . . like she would hold up ink blots and ask me what it was and I would say a butterfly and she would say "interesting." But it wasn't like that.

One week, she asked me about my grandparents. I started talking about my Grandma Lucy. I felt this big ball in my stomach. I thought I was going to throw up. Then I just started crying.

Grandma Lucy and I were best friends, because my parents traveled so much. It seems like every day of my life we were together.

We had planned to go to the park on a Thursday morning to have a breakfast picnic and watch the people walk their dogs. On that Thursday morning, I ran into her room to wake her up, but she wouldn't wake up. She must have died in her sleep. I had learned at school about calling 911. I laid there next to her until the police came. I didn't cry.

I was so mad. We had plans. We had so many things we were going to do. And she just left. She didn't show up. She was gone.

Anyway, the counselor said I was mad about Grandma Lucy all this time, not all these other things. She said I needed to decide to let Grandma Lucy go.

So here I am, Grandma Lucy *(BENDING DOWN)*. I have to let you go. I love you, and I will always miss you. But I'm not mad anymore. You had to go. That's just how it is. But I know I'll see you again.

So be happy when you watch me from heaven, *(PAUSE)* because I'm deciding to be happy, too.

STEPHANIE'S FRIEND

Regina Moore

I am *really* mad at my sister. She said she doesn't want me hanging around Stephanie anymore. She says she is a bad influence on me. I understand she is concerned, but doesn't she trust me? I know I am younger, but I have some common sense.

I know Stephanie is different than me. She has a Mom, no Dad. She told me he left before she was born and she hasn't really ever had anyone in her life that she could look up to like a father. She's always dating older guys. Maybe that's *why* I want to be her friend. If she doesn't have someone to show her a better way of acting or dressing, she'll never understand anything but what she knows now. I want her to see that she can be better than how she sees herself.

I just want to be her friend. She needs somebody there for her while she is trying to figure things out.

CELL PHONE
Regina Moore

I promise, if you get me a cell phone I will do whatever you ask.

(*HESITATE*)

I know I said I would wash dishes if you bought me those shoes. And I did . . . for two whole weeks! That was last year, Mom. I have matured since then. I feel like I am ready for the responsibility.

I will be very careful. I won't lose it because I know cell phones are expensive.

Becca's mom let *her* have a cell phone. Her mom told her it was so she could stay in touch with her. If I had a cell phone, you could reach me at all times. It would be like you were with me even when you weren't.

I could do chores to help pay the cell phone bill. I could do babysitting for the Bartholmew's or I could do a yard sale. Please, Mom, *everyone* my age has a cell phone except me. I am asking you to have mercy on me. Without a cell phone, you will make me an orphan in every social setting.

I have *dreams*, Mom. I want to be the student body president one day. I could be the captain of the cheerleading squad or homecoming queen, but if I am an outcast, I haven't got a chance in life. Mom, my future depends on it. Please, I am *begging* you. If you truly love me you will let me have a cell phone.

LEMONADE

Regina Moore

I think I've had it. It's too hot out here.

Yeah, I know; I'm supposed to be selling lemonade. But the ice is melting faster than I can sell it. Mom said I could make some money to buy new DVD's. She acted like it was going to be so easy.

First, I had to get up early to make the lemonade. I thought I could use the instant stuff, but mom insisted on the real thing. Do you know how long it takes to squeeze forty-seven lemons?

I was afraid I wouldn't have enough plastic cups. Well, I was wrong. I've had two people stop by: Mrs. Caruthers taking a walk on her walker and Jerry Spencer from across the street. He still hasn't paid me for the first glass!

Well, it's getting close to lunchtime. Maybe I'll have a mad rush. It's *definitely* getting hotter. Maybe I'll catch the guys down the street when they finish playing basketball. Mr. and Mrs. Miller will probably want a drink after working in their yard.

Oh, wait. Here comes someone!

(PAUSE)

Hi, mom.

Well, money is money.

BEST FRIENDS FOREVER

Cali Elizabeth Moore

When you say "Best Friends Forever" in the 3RD grade, it doesn't mean too much. I mean, as soon as you want to be the same thing on Halloween, the friendship is over. But with Heather and I . . . I just thought it would be different.

Heather moved to Smithville when we were in the 3RD grade. The first day of school, the teacher assigned her the seat next to mine. After that, we were inseparable. My mom even said we were "attached at the hip." We were like the same person.

Actually, we were more like sisters. We liked the same music, the same TV shows, the same clothes, and never the same guy. It was perfect. We had sleepovers that would start as just one night and end up being a week. We just never got tired of laughing together.

Even in the rough times, we were there for each other. When her grandmother died, we had a sleepover and watched home movies and talked about her grandmother until we fell asleep. And when my parents started fighting a lot, I stayed at her house and we watched scary movies.

But one day, things changed. After six years, something just broke in our friendship. It was weird. I can't pin point the exact time or moment, but we just started falling apart.

One day I invited her to go eat and see a movie, but she was busy. The next day I called to see if she wanted to spend the night that weekend; she said she had some family stuff to do.

At first, honestly, I didn't catch that she was just ignoring me. I thought she really *was* busy three weekends in row. I thought she really *was* too tired to talk on the phone. I thought she really *did* have to get to class early and *didn't* have time to talk in the hall. But that wasn't the truth.

The truth was she met a girl named Kara in her fifth period class. They started to hang out a lot. When Heather had to get to class early, she was going to Kara's locker to talk. And all the times she was too tired to talk on the phone, she was talking to Kara on the other line.

I just couldn't believe it. Heather had never lied to me before . . . had she? I couldn't be certain now. I mean,

I didn't care if she hung out with other people, but why was she being sneaky? It just wasn't like her.

I decided to ask Heather what was going on. I went to her house one day after school. I just surprised her and showed up. I had been rehearsing what I would say, but nothing sounded right. I mean, how do you confront your best friend?

When I got to Heather's house, she was surprised to see me. I came in and we started talking about school and stuff, almost like everything was okay. But it wasn't. Finally, I told her that I knew she'd been hanging out with Kara a lot. I also told her that I knew she hung out with Kara when she told me she was busy, or tired, or had family plans. She said Kara understood her better than I did. Then she told me something I thought I'd never hear her say. She said, "Kara is my best friend now. Kara and I smoke weed and you would never do that. And she thinks it is okay and so do I. She doesn't freak out about getting drunk, either."

My world stared spinning. I couldn't believe that she had changed so much! We had always talked about how we thought that drinking and drugs were wrong. Now she is doing them both with NO remorse!

I told her that I would always care about her, but that I was not going to change what I believe to be her friend. I walked out of Heather's house and started to cry.

It's easy to say you'll never let anyone change who you are or what you believe when no one has ever tried. I think it would have been easier if it had been anyone but Heather. Somehow I did it, though. I walked out of that door knowing I'd lost a friend, but gained worth.

I still see Heather at school sometimes. We smile and wave. Of course it's not the same, and that can be hard to deal with. Heather gets in trouble a lot now and is dating a guy who isn't too nice to her. I want to be there for her, but I know she doesn't want my help.

I know that Heather and I aren't best friends anymore. But, in a way, we are. Because no matter what, for six years, she was the best friend I've ever had.

THE SPORTY GROUP

Cali Elizabeth Moore

Okay. So there are lots of "groups" at school.

You know—the super smart ones, the artsy ones, the band kids, the ones who sleep all day, you know. It's cool because if you're in a group, you stand out at school. I want to be known as sporty. There is just one catch: I'm completely uncoordinated.

I tried out for tennis and got caught in the net. I don't know how, but I did. I looked like a butterfly with a broken wing just kicking around in circles.

I thought maybe basketball would be better. Well, my head had more contact with the ball than my hands. I actually got knocked out by the ball while someone was passing it to me.

This made me think that maybe I'm better with my feet. So, you guessed it: I tried soccer. I don't even want to talk about that one. Let's just say I got the nickname "grass face" from the first day of tryouts.

So I don't know if the sporty title is going to work out for ole' grass face *(POINTS TO HERSELF)*.

Maybe I could be part of the ordinary-kids-who-don't-stand-out-and-are-cool-with-it group. That sounds pretty good right now.

MY OWN ROOM

Cali Elizabeth Moore

There is only one thing I want. There is only thing I need to make my life happy and peaceful. It may seem like a silly request, but my sanity depends on it. I need my own room!

I share a room with the messiest, loudest, most nosy, smelly person I've ever known. This catastrophe's name is Holly, and she is my sister. She does things that would make grown men cry.

Holly likes to throw her clothes from her closet to the floor so she can see them better. I guess she likes the convenience of rolling out of bed and picking up whatever is on the floor, putting it on, and going to school. I personally think that's disgusting.

And don't even get me *started* on loud. I mean, the kind of obnoxious loud that makes your ears ring! She sings songs she doesn't know the words to, and to top it off, she is so off key sometimes I don't even know what song it is. She also talks, like, seven notches louder than any other person I've met. Mom is always saying, "Holly, turn it down. I'm right here." It's like she's speaking to a crowd of thousands when I'm just sitting next to her in the car.

But worst of all is the sneaky, spying, nosy side of Holly, the side that only I see. She goes through all of my stuff: diaries, jean pockets, yearbooks . . . she even listens in on my phone conversations. And she doesn't keep it to herself. If she finds something juicy, everyone knows before I get to school the next day. I can't have a crush or dislike someone or copy someone's homework or live my life without EVERYONE knowing about it!

She's driving me crazy. I know I have some kind of rights. Something has to be done. If not for me, then for big sisters everywhere.

So Mom, stop this madness. I need my own room. I rest my case.

FASHION DESIGNER

Cali Elizabeth Moore

When I'm older, I am going to be a full-time fashion designer. Obviously! For now, school is taking up a lot of my time. I mean, I have *tons* of style. All my friends try to "borrow" my clothes so they can dress just like me. They never want to give them back, but who can blame them?

My brother says that it's for my own good that they steal my clothes. He says they are hideous and I dress like a homeless person. I personally feel sorry for him, though. I think he is blind to real fashion when he sees it and *that* is truly a shame.

Just last week, I was at the mall with my mom and a woman said to my mom, "Your daughter is darling." That day I was wearing a blue skirt with a blue and white striped top from one of my favorite stores: Jungle Beach. It's a great place for cutting edge fashion. I said, "It's from Jungle Beach." She laughed and said, "Kids say the craziest things!" Whatever *that* means.

I also make clothes, only my mom doesn't let me

use the sewing machine, so I have to use fabric glue. Therefore, everything is . . . well . . . shabby chic. I use a lot of torn fabric and beads. It's going to be the new thing this spring. I saw it in *Teen Vogue*.

Anyway, I have a fashion show next week in celebration of my new handbag line. They are a mix of Louise V and Dior. You'll really love them, so I encourage you to attend.

THE BATH
Regina Moore

I wish my little brother would take a bath. I bet the last time he took a bath was last week. My dog, Rex, gets more baths than he does. Mom is always yelling, "Matthew, get out of the mud puddles!" That's what a five year old boy likes to do. He likes to do finger painting and you can imagine what a mess he makes doing that. Of course, Mom thinks it is adorable. She says he is expressing his "creative talents." I think it gives him permission to get really messy. Oh, and of *course* he doesn't get in trouble.

Is it a little boy thing? Do little boys *have* to get dirty because they are boys? Well, *I* think so. I know Matthew and he can't help it. He was just born to ride his bike in the rain, to drop food on the kitchen floor, to put candy in his pocket before mom washes his clothes, to blow his nose on Dad's tie, to stick his hand in my plate because he wants the last ear of corn, to . . . do you understand my situation here?

This is probably okay for a little while longer, but when he gets older no one will want to come over to stay the night. And when he leaves home to go to college, it will be difficult for him to find a roommate. No girl will want to date him so he will never get married. Being messy could ruin his whole life!

But wait . . . Mom says Dad is a slob. He can't keep the garage clean and she says all she does is pick up after him. Hey, maybe it isn't Matthew's fault at all. He has two things against him that he can't control: he's a boy and he is *just* like Dad.

Now that I think about it, I kind of feel sorry for my brother. It's like being born with a sickness!

Everything Happens for a Reason

Cali Elizabeth Moore

My mom always said that everything happens for a reason. I always thought she said that because it ends a conversation. I can't really complain when she's told me everything in the universe is connected, so I should just deal with it. But within the past month, I've realized that there might be something real behind what she's always told me.

Last Monday, my brother Todd wasn't feeling well. They sent him home from school. Mom made him minestrone soup, because it's his favorite. He slept all day.

When my sister and I got home, we joked with Todd like we always do. I told him he was faking sick and that I was going to tell Mom. He laughed, but he wasn't really smiling. I could tell he was really sick.

The next day my sister and I went to school, but Todd didn't. He was still sick.

That afternoon, Grandma came to pick my sister and me up from school. I was surprised because Grandma lives in Florida and no one said she was coming.

The whole ride home was silent.

When we got home, Mom and Dad were there. They were sitting in the living room. The TV was off. Mom and Dad told us to sit down. They told us that Todd was really sick. The kind of sick that doesn't get better.

(PAUSE)

They said Todd was going to die. The doctor said he may not make it through the week. For now, he was resting upstairs.

My sister started to cry. I didn't, though. I felt like I was dreaming, or like someone was playing a mean joke.

For the next two days, my family didn't go to school or work or anything. All we did was spend time together. We watched old home movies and looked through family albums. We ate ice cream at 2:00 A.M. and took a hot air balloon ride. It was amazing . . . and sad.

One day, Todd got so sick he couldn't stay at home anymore. He had to be on oxygen. That's when we heard about the Smithson's.

The Smithson's were a family from Connecticut. They had a daughter named Andrea. Andrea was sick like Todd, except she could be cured. Andrea needed a new heart. The doctor said that Andrea and Todd had the same blood type. Todd said that when he died, he wanted Andrea to have his heart.

At first I couldn't believe he would say that. He wasn't going to *die*! He was just sick. He would feel better soon and then everything would go back to normal.

But then, Friday afternoon, my brother Todd died.

I was in shock for a long time. I couldn't believe he was gone. He was in my life every day I can remember since I was born. I got angry, too, but mostly I just missed him. I felt like I was drowning, but then something changed. I met Andrea.

Andrea came with her family to visit my family. She was so nice and funny. She was appreciative and caring . . . and she had Todd's heart.

I can't believe my brother is gone. But I *can* believe he would do something this wonderful for someone else. And the truth is, everything happens for a reason.

KRISTI'S BATHROOM

Regina Moore

Hey Mom, I need to talk to you. Kristi's going to be leaving to go to college, so her room is going to be available . . . and her bathroom. I know Jeff is older than me, but Kristi's room has its own bathroom. It would take care of all of our problems if you just give me her room. Jeff is always saying that I spend too much time in the bathroom.

Well, if I had Kristi's room, I would not have to use the hallway bathroom. No more pantyhose hanging from the shower rack, rollers and curling irons on the cabinet. Come *on*, Mom. You remember what it was like to share a bathroom with a boy and everyone else that comes into your house.

What?

You mean . . . you'll consider it? Mom, you're the *best*! I told all my friends that you'd understand. Now that I know that *you* know this is a life or death situation, I have to confess: I can't live another day sharing a bathroom with Jeff.

DRIVER'S TEST

Regina Moore

I've waited a long time for this day. I have been sitting out here for an hour.

Today, I am taking my driver's test.

I guess I should go in. I am kind of nervous, but I am excited, too. Mom won't have to drive me to school or to my friends' houses. Dad said I will have to get a job to help pay for my gas and car insurance. I could get a job at the sub shop after school and still have time to do my homework. Mom and Dad said that I still have to keep my grades up, so that I can keep my car keys.

I hope I pass the test. Carter, next door, failed his test twice before he got his license. I've been studying for three months. Carter said it helps if you get a nice driving instructor. I hope I don't get nervous and forget something like what to do at a railroad crossing. I just can't worry about it. I have studied and now I have to just take the test.

Hey, wait—are they locking the door? I thought it said they were open until 6:00 P.M. in the driver's manual.

Well, I guess I had better read the book again just to make sure I haven't overlooked anything. I will have to come back tomorrow. What's one more day?

REMARRIED

Cali Elizabeth Moore

Do you ever feel like you're the adult and your parents are the children? Well, that is what I have been dealing with for the past six months. My mother has been acting like a lovesick teenager. I swear she thinks every love song is about her!

See, my mom is getting remarried to this guy named Bill. Bill is a tax attorney and they met at the grocery store. But to hear her tell the story of the way they met, you'd think doves were released and violins were playing in aisle nine of the grocery store.

I mean, don't get me wrong. I like Bill. He's nice enough. He tries to be nice to my brother and me. And he *really* likes Mom. I can tell.

It's just ridiculous the way they are acting while planning this wedding. They have both been married before and they aren't just a couple of young kids with nothing but love to keep them alive! I mean, come on!

My mom wants to have a huge wedding and invite everyone she knows and get an expensive wedding dress and have my Aunt Tina sing "Endless Love." It just kind of makes me sick. I mean . . . it's just . . . she's already been married, you know, to MY dad! Remember? And now she's going to invite all the same people that came to *that* wedding to her *next* one? It's like saying, "I know the last one failed, but I think I got it this time."

I don't know. Maybe I'm being a little harsh or something. I just feel a little embarrassed. I want her to be happy and I'm glad she is. I just wish she could think about how this is affecting me.

You know?

MAKING THE SQUAD

Regina Moore

Have you seen the list? I haven't seen it, but they said they would put the list out on the bulletin board today. I wonder who made the cheerleading squad. This is the first year they have allowed the football team to have a cheerleading squad. And they said if the girls could add something to the athletic department, they could cheer for the basketball team, too.

I hope I made the team. I really want to be on the cheerleading squad for a hundred reasons, but mainly because my best friends are trying out, too. Kate and Jamie are used to making the list. It seems like everything they try out for, they make it.

I used to be a junior pro cheerleader when I was younger. I've been in dance since I was two and I have been a gymnast for the last five years. I feel like I am pretty; maybe not gorgeous, but very pretty. I think I look as good as any of the other girls. I know I can dance and do the jumps. I have a very good memory, so I know I can remember the cheers. I went through the tryouts in my head, over and over.

I walked out to the center of the gym floor. I smiled really big, but very natural. I did the cheer. I did the triple front handspring and landed it perfectly. I don't think I left anything out. Did I thank the judges when I walked away? I thought I did. Oh, I'm sure I did. Oh no, I'm not sure if I thanked the judges. You're supposed to *always* thank the judges. Even if you think you did a terrible job, you thank the judges.

Well, I probably didn't make it. I can't believe it. I prepared for years for that very moment and I made one mistake that may have cost me the spot on the squad.

The judges know me. They saw me smiling. They know I wouldn't be rude. Miss Daniel's is the librarian. I always talk to her. Mr. Robins is the basketball coach and my history teacher. I always make good grades in his class and turn in extra work. The only other judge I really didn't know is that lady from the new dance studio. She seemed nice. She told me nice job on my jumps.

(DEEP BREATH) I did the best I could.

Is the list up? Can I see?

(READING ALOUD)

Jamie Simmons, Lindsay Lee, Latoya Caldwell. She was really good. Beth Barker. And me.

I made it! I'm so excited. I made it! I can't wait to tell Claire! I guess we'll have to cheer up Kate. It's too bad she didn't make the team.

Well, all you can do is work hard, do your best, and believe that if it's meant to be, it will happen.

You know, don't stress over it.

PART 3
Boys

As we wrote these monologues for boys, we felt it was important to deal with a wide range of experiences: the driving test, new jobs, relationships with everyone from girls to parents. There are fewer boys in this industry than girls, and the right materials can give them a great edge.

When delivering the monologues, be sure not to move through them too quickly. Choose selections that can be delivered like a real story of something that happened recently, with all of the emotions and mannerisms you would feel in the same situation.

THE DANCE TRAGEDY

Cali Elizabeth Moore

I can't believe this! Of all the nights to be a complete idiot, I just *had* to pick this one!

(*PAUSES AND WAVES LIKE HE IS ENJOYING HIMSELF*)

I finally got up the nerve to ask Sarah Davenport to the end of the year dance. And for some reason, God only knows why, she said "yes." I am at the dance right now with the captain of the cheerleading squad, the most popular girl in school. Sarah Davenport! But, of course, as fate would have it, tragedy has already struck.

You see, I got really nervous when we first got here. I mean, the whole school is here. Everyone saw Sarah and I walk in together! I got her some punch and then she said she had to go to the bathroom, so Sarah and five of her friends went to the bathroom. I knew this was the moment. She would either tell them she really liked me or she'd fake sick and leave. This scenario made me short of breath, so I went to get a little air.

I walked over here to these air conditioning units and took some deep breaths. I started to feel better, so I turned to head back to the refreshment table when I realized something: *MY SHIRT WAS STUCK IN THE AIR CONDITIONING UNIT!*

It has been two hours now! Sarah has come over and hinted that she wants to dance three times! I just keep telling her that we'll dance when a better song comes on. Oh, by the way, I am freezing. I seriously think I'm catching a cold over here!

I only have two choices: rip the shirt and look like Tarzan all night, or stay here till the dance is over and the janitor comes in and turns thing off.

Well *(LEANING BACK IN A MORE COMFORTABLE POSITION)*, it looks like it's going to be a long night.

THE LAST LETTER
Regina Moore

I was going through my grandfather's boxes in the attic because they are moving his things out of the old house. I found something. I found a chest of old photos and some letters he wrote my grandmother. He fought in Vietnam and he wrote letters to her every day. He told her about the friends he fought with and the places they went.

The letters talked about his assignments and the beauty of the country. Sometimes he wrote about how much he missed her and how he couldn't wait to see her again. I found so many letters, but at the bottom of the chest there was a letter that had not been opened. I asked my grandmother why she didn't open it. She told me it was three weeks before he was supposed to come home, when they were ambushed. She got the news that he had been killed two weeks later. She said it didn't seem real. She couldn't believe he wasn't coming home. Then, a week later, on the day he was supposed to come home, she got a letter: a letter from Grandpa. She said she almost opened his last letter.

She had been saving it all this time. She smiled at me, and told me to open it. I opened it and began to read:

> *To my sweet Karla,*
>
> *I count the days until I see you again. We are anticipating standing on American soil and seeing those we love. I do believe we have made a difference. I have learned about the importance of fighting for what you believe in and never looking back. I will not look back and only look to spending the rest of my life with you.*

Grandma smiled and said he *did* come home.

I never met my grandfather, but I like to think I am just like him.

(*PAUSE*)

I really hope I can come close.

Scarlet Fever

Cali Elizabeth Moore

My best friend Will is really loosing it. I mean, I have been friends with Will since we were five years old. I've seen him do some pretty crazy stuff. But this tops it all.

Will has a girlfriend. Her name is Scarlet. She sits next to him in class. She has long brown hair and blue eyes. And Will says he is in love!

Now, I have tried to convince him otherwise, but he just won't listen. He says, "There is no cure for what I've got."

(PAUSE)

What does that even mean?

All he talks about now is Scarlet. "Scarlet is so pretty ," and "Guess what Scarlet said," and "Scarlet likes that, too." I think *I* know more about Scarlet than *Scarlet* knows about Scarlet.

The worst part is that everything we do is interrupted by Scarlet. We go to a movie; Scarlet has to come. I go to his house for dinner; he spends the whole time talking to Scarlet on the phone. And . . . well, you get the picture.

I just can't take it anymore. I don't know what to do! She's a nice girl, but if I have to hear one more random fact about her, I think I am going to scream!

Isn't there a cure for Scarlet fever?

CLASS CLOWN NO MORE

Cali Elizabeth Moore

Everyone knows I'm the funniest kid in class.

I make everyone laugh when we are supposed to be quiet. I wear funny shirts with sayings on them like "If I were any hotter I'd melt," or the classic "If you're reading this you need a new hobby." It's common knowledge that *I* am the class clown.

But now, all the kids in class are acting like this new kid is funnier than me. ME! The guy who came to school on tacky day dressed like Principal Smithson. I mean, *come on*! No one can compete with that!

They all say, "Oh, Steven, you're so funny" just because he pretends to slam his hand in door. It's such amateur comedy. I did that stuff *two years* ago!

The teachers are buying into it, too. When Steven's mom came to pick him up from school yesterday, Mrs. Brown told his mother he was "such a riot." That's what she used to say to *my* mom.

Well, I'm tired of not being noticed! I'm going to change my title around the class if class clown has been stolen from me.

From now on, I'm William the Stinky Kid!

GUYS NIGHT OUT

Cali Elizabeth Moore

Tonight I've decided: it's time for a night out. I need a night with just me and the guys.

See, I'm a committed man. My girlfriend's name is Whitney, and we've been together for three months. She's great! She's got long brown hair and big blue eyes. We have a ton in common.

The thing is *(PAUSE)*, sometimes a man just needs time away from his woman. You know, to experience all life has to offer. I need a night to be rough and untamed and dangerous. And that night is tonight.

I told Whitney we needed to take the night off because I had "guy stuff" to take care of. She was kind of upset. We had already planned to go ice skating. But there was no turning back now. This man had put his foot down.

Any minute now, the guys will be picking me up for a night on the town. We'll probably go bowling or to the county fair first. Later, when things get crazy, we'll go to John's back yard and have a paintball war: at night.

I guess Whitney will find something to do tonight.

She could go hang out at Sara's house. Sara is Whitney's best friend. Maybe they'll go to the mall or something. If they go to the football game, they may run into Whitney's ex-boyfriend, Steven. He's still likes her. I know it.

Steven is one of those jock guys. He plays football and basketball and baseball and any other sport you can think of that I didn't already say. They went out for about seven months.

(PAUSE)

She probably won't go to the football game.

You know, I'm actually tired. I don't think I'll go out with the guys tonight. I'd like to watch a movie at home. Maybe I'll call Whitney to come over and watch a movie with me. I wouldn't want to make her stay home alone all night long.

Dad Changed

Cali Elizabeth Moore

My dad is what you would call a "Man's Man." Not just any kind of man's man, though. He loves watching football, hanging out with "the guys," playing golf, and doing some "hard core cardio." I guess you could say in the past year he really has become a new man. And to be honest, it's kind of ridiculous.

He wasn't always this way. Just one day, Dad started saying things like "Yo buddy, what up?" or "Cool, peace out." At first, I didn't mind. I just thought he was joking around or trying to prove a point. He hasn't stopped, though. And I'm getting a little freaked out. It's kind of embarrassing when he says "Greg in the house" as he walks into the room at a parent teacher conference.

Dad's change in personality came soon after he bought a new car. It's pretty cool, too. It's really fast and red. The top comes down on it. The license plate says "TOO HOT."

Mom says we couldn't afford that car. Mom seems to have a whole theory on the matter. She says he's going through some kind of "mid-life crisis." I don't really understand what that means. Every time he says something about his car or tries to talk in that funny way, she just rolls her eyes. She says he needs to "get over himself."

Personally, I think dad just wants to be more appealing to me. And honestly, it's working. We listen to the same music now. We like the same cars. He even keeps up with celebrity gossip. But something is missing.

I can't really describe it, but . . . well . . . I kind of miss the old Dad. The Dad who listened to the Eagles and the best of Fleetwood Mac. The Dad who swore that nothing ran quite like a 69' Ford pick-up. Is it weird to say you miss your dad when he hasn't gone anywhere?

ETHAN'S MONOLOGUE

Cali Elizabeth Moore

Have you ever tried really hard to do something and no matter how hard you try, you just can't? Well, maybe you haven't. Maybe everything is easy for you. It is for some people. But it's not for me.

I have been in the same grade for three years. *Three years!* I have tried, I really have, but I am no good at school. And trust me, I've heard it all. The old "everybody's good at something" line does not apply to me. I am a mess with math. I can't spell. I hate books and it takes me an embarrassing amount of time to read one. I can't remember anything in history. I'm good at nothing.

The worst part is, my parents just keep on believing in me. I know that doesn't sound bad, but it is. They tell me over and over how smart I am and how this next report card will be different, but it never is. Every time I come home with another "F, " they sigh and say, "Next time Ethan."

But it's not next time. It's not going to be next time.

I'm not the kid they think I am. I'm not smart and it's embarrassing. Not just to me, but I'm sure to them. They act like they're so proud, but I know they aren't. What parent wants to tell their friends that this year their son is in the same grade . . . again?

(PAUSE)

Sometimes I just feel trapped. I feel like I'll be in the same grade forever, with everyone saying, "Just keep trying." But what if I just can't try anymore?

BAD HAIR CUT

Cali Elizabeth Moore

I am never taking this hat off, okay? I might as well just glue it to my head. I am going to eat, sleep, and shower in this hat. You will never see me with it off. Truth be told, I *hate* this hat. But I hate my new hair cut more.

This morning, my dad took me to get my hair cut. He said he had been going to this place for years. That should have been my first clue that something wasn't right. Then, when I sat down in the chair, the lady cutting my hair said she wanted to turn me away from the mirror so I would be surprised when she was done. Let's just say I was surprised. No, I was *shocked*.

Anyway, I put this hat on because it was the first thing I could find in the car. If a trash bag or my backpack had been closer to me, it would be on my head right now. I just wanted to cover up whatever is going on up on top of my head.

How am I going to go to school? Teachers don't allow hats. I'm going to have to fake sick until it grows back or something. If anyone sees this . . . if Amy sees this, she'll break up with me for sure!

Okay. Action needs to be taken. I'm just going to have to use some of dad's hair growing gel. He puts it on his bald spot. Maybe it will make my hair grow back by Monday.

This is for you Amy! *(RUNS OFF)*

THE CORN MAZE

Cali Elizabeth Moore

I give up! I have been walking through this corn maze for an hour and a half and there is no end! I should never have come in the first place. I hate mazes! I got lost once in the jungle gym at a fast food restaurant for two hours when I was six. The only reason I'm here is because of Kayla.

Kayla said a whole bunch of people were going to the corn maze tonight at school. I thought, "Perfect! This will be my chance to be with Kayla." So I told her I'd be there.

Well, I was planning on leading Kayla away from the group so we could talk and then she'd get scared in the dark and grab my arm and we'd gaze into each other's eyes and have one of those moments where you just know this is the beginning of something big . . . didn't happen. When I got her away from the group, we ran into a ghost or something. I really don't know *what* it was, to be honest, but we were just walking and I felt a hand on my shoulder and I just started running. I heard

Kayla behind yelling, "Come back, come back!" Later I realized she was only saying "come back" because I have the flashlight.

So now I'm the loser who left Kayla Justice in a corn maze without a flashlight. And to top it all off, I don't know if I'll ever make it out of here.

I'll never eat corn again.

It's Over

Cali Elizabeth Moore

Last night my girlfriend broke up with me. We had been dating for two years. I know that doesn't seem like a lot. I mean, I'm just in high school. But most high school relationships last a month. My dad's second marriage didn't last two years.

Everything was going so great. Jessica, my girlfriend, used to always come over after school and we'd go swimming at the neighborhood pool. She's so smart. She always helped me with my homework. In the winter, we'd go ice skating. I play hockey, so I'm pretty good at skating. Jessica is horrible, though. She'd leave with bruises all over her knees.

I was pretty close to her family, too. I went out to eat with them a lot. Sometimes I'd take her brother to soccer practice when her parents were busy. I even went over to their house on Thanksgiving and Easter for the last two years.

It's just weird to think of her not around. We spent a lot of time together. We have all the same friends. We hang out at all the same places. We even have a couple of classes together.

Jessica said she didn't want to be tied down. She wanted more time with her friends. I guess I understand. But we didn't have to break up over that. We could have just not hung out so much. I mean, that's two years of my life down the drain. We both put a lot into the relationship.

And what will everyone think at school? All of our friends used to joke with us about how we were going to get married. We were voted cutest couple! Everyone is going to be talking about the break up. Everyone is going to be asking me about it. I won't be able to get away from it.

Then there'll be the awkwardness. Do we talk, do we not talk? Do we hug, do we not hug? What if she cries? What if *I* cry?

I wonder if she's even upset. She's probably out with her friends right now enjoying her freedom. They're at the movies or having a sleepover or at the mall. She's having fun. Why would she cry over me and our two year relationship?

Okay, so this is it. I can't act upset anymore. I have to just tough this out and deal with it.

(PAUSE)

It's over.

It's over.

It's really over.

YARD SALE

Regina Moore

I don't know *what* she is thinking. I went to my friend's house Saturday morning and when I got home, half of my room was in the front yard along with a giant "Yard Sale" sign. She must be crazy if she thinks I'm letting her sell some of this stuff!

Dad gave me some of his old records that are pretty cool. Stuff like the Beatles and ZZ Top. He said they'd be worth something in a few years. So I put them in a box in the garage. Well, they aren't in a box in the garage anymore. They're on a table labeled "Five dollars or less." *FIVE DOLLARS OR LESS!*

And what about my bike? I mean, I haven't used it in a couple of years, but it's still *my* bike. This isn't right.

(*MOTIONING TO CORNER*)

There is some little kid trying out my skateboard. He has no idea what he is doing. He's going to break it. I can't watch.

BUSTED

Cali Elizabeth Moore

Hello, Officer. First, I would just like to say that I understand you are doing your job by pulling me over and I respect that. You keep our streets safe and I am in your debt. Second, here are my license, registration, and proof of insurance. I think you will find that they are all in order as they should be. I am a law-abiding citizen. You may notice when you run my tags that I have no prior record. This is because I have never been pulled over before and I have never been charged for any other crime. Third, I want to fess up now and make you aware that I did have a poppy seed bagel for breakfast this morning and I read online that poppy seed can make you breathe a higher score on a breathalyzer test. I just wanted to let you know I have not been drinking, only partaking in a delicious breakfast food.

(LONG PAUSE)

Do I know why you pulled me over? Do I know why you pulled me . . . ? *(LOOKING AROUND FRANTICALLY)*

Well, I signaled. I stopped at the red light. I merged

properly. I'm not a fugitive on the run. I'm not a member of the mafia or an underground drug ring. I don't own a gun. I haven't kidnapped anyone.

(PAUSE) Is this about my bumper sticker? I didn't realize it was a traffic violation to ask people to "honk if they love elves." Please don't take me to jail! Do you know what they'll do to a guy like me in the big house? *Do you?*

(LONG PAUSE; HYPERVENTILATING)

Excuse me? *(BREATHING HARD)* You pulled me over because my tail light is out? That's *it*? Why didn't you say so? I'll get it taken care of right away.

(LONG PAUSE)

Yes! Yes, Officer! I will. I'll be safe. Thanks for letting me off the hook this time.

(YELLING OUT THE WINDOW; THE OFFICER IS ALREADY GONE)

I appreciate all you do for the community! You're a beacon of hope in a world of darkness!

(TO HIMSELF) Whew, that was close!

A REAL FAMILY

Regina Moore

I really liked this place. I guess I've liked them all, but this one was my favorite. Something about this one . . . really felt like home.

I made a lot of new friends at the school here, especially Heath. Heath and I sit next to each other in class. Heath and I were becoming good friends. We may have been best friends. It doesn't matter now.

I had a big brother here, too. Not a real one, but it felt like it. We would all go to his football games on Friday nights at the high school. He's really fast. He made three touchdowns in the same game! Sometimes early on Saturday mornings he would come into my room and wake me up. He'd say, "Let's work on that arm." We'd go outside on the front lawn and throw the football till breakfast was ready.

I think I'll miss my mom and dad the most, though. They were the best parents I've ever had. We did a lot of fun things together, but that's not what I liked best.

It was like I knew they cared about me. They would

ask me about my day and help me with my homework. Mom would make pancakes with a syrup smiley face. It was like they wanted me to be happy.

I just can't understand why it didn't work out here. The social worker says that it's nobody's fault; it's just that sometimes you're not a good fit. But that's the thing . . . we were a *perfect* fit. Strangers would even say things like, "You have your daddy's eyes" or "You have your mother's smile." We looked like a family. We even felt like a real family.

So why couldn't we be one?

July 3RD

Cali Elizabeth Moore

When my parents told me I was going to be a big brother, I was pretty excited. I mean, I was kind of young, but I knew that it meant someone to play with. It sounded great!

I was wrong.

On July 3RD, a baby was born to my household. A baby . . . GIRL! I couldn't believe it. The thought had never crossed my mind. A baby *sister*? Now what?

I'll tell you "now what"! No more being loud in the house, the guest bedroom is painted pink, and *lots* of bows and dresses. That's right. We're talking a complete turnaround.

I was so happy. I thought that this was my big chance. I thought this would be my best friend for life. Boy was *I* wrong. She can't even talk!

Dad says that she will learn to talk and that she'll want to play. He says soon I can teach her how to build forts and play video games. He says she can "learn from a pro."

I guess he's right. I mean, I'll get over not having a brother eventually.

And just think of all the things she'll need to learn from me. Like fishing, swimming, what not to eat at Grandma's . . . .

You know, this might not be so bad.

COLLEGE

Cali Elizabeth Moore

When you're a senior in high school, it can be hard to decide where you want to go to college. There are so many colleges to choose from, and you want to go where your friends are going, too. But it has been ten times harder for me to decide, because I don't *have* a choice.

My dad went to Hale University, and in his mind, there is nowhere else *to* go. He has been dreaming of me going there my whole life. We went on our first campus tour when I was ten years old. It's all he talks about. But I don't want to go to Hale University.

I have been checking out colleges for the last three years and I found one I really like. It's called Jones Technical College. It has great classes for Photography and that is what I think I want to do. I love the campus and a few of my friends are going there.

(*PAUSE*)

This is a letter from Jones Technical College and inside it is my fate. I've had this envelope for a week and I just can't open it. If this letter says I got in, I will have to pay my way through college. Dad says he won't pay for a second rate education, and to him that's anywhere that isn't Hale.

Ok I'm just going to do it.

(OPENS THE ENVELOPE; PULLS LETTER OUT)

(PAUSE)

That's okay. Hale won't be so bad.

At least Dad will be happy.

LADIES' MAN

Cali Elizabeth Moore

I guess you could say I'm a ladies' man. The ladies love me. And it's not my fault. They're always saying, "John, you're so handsome," or "John, you're so strong." I guess I am.

When I was just a young boy, my dad told me, "Son, this family is cursed. We are too good looking. Because of this curse, girls will flock to us from miles around just to witness how masculine we are." I didn't quite understand then. But now it's clear.

Yesterday at school, Kara Burton passed a note to me in class. In the note, Kara confessed her two-year crush on me. She spoke of my kindness and, of course, my good looks. The "I's" were dotted with hearts. She spelled my name James instead of John, though. I found that strangely ironic since there is a boy named James who sits right next to me.

Just this morning, I was going to water my mother's flowers when I noticed a group of girls coming to the door. They had matching green outfits on and they had a few boxes of cookies. By the time I had gotten inside, the girls were gone and there were several boxes of cookies on the kitchen counter. One could only conclude that the girls were admirers and had left a simple gift of cookies.

It's amazing. These things happen to me all the time. Almost every day is turned into an extraordinary day just because I am a charming, sophisticated gentleman. And who could complain?

THE SKI BOAT

Regina Moore

Mom, did you see what Dad brought home? It is the last thing you would ever guess. Go ahead, guess.

Okay, Okay, I'll tell you. Dad bought a boat. That's right, a *boat*. Not a canoe. It's bigger. It isn't a fishing boat, Mom, it's a ski boat!

That's right. Remember when Dad said he wanted to teach me to ski? Well, it looks like he is finally going to do it.

Wait until I tell Mark! He's always bragging about his dad's motorcycle and how they take trips together. I can't wait to learn to ski, so I can invite him to the lake. He'll probably act like he can ski and then fall in the water over and over. For once I'll be able to do something he can't do! And I'm going to rub it in, too!

A ski boat! Can you believe it?

(*PAUSE*)

Why is Dad pulling into the driveway next door? Wait, why is Dad giving Mark's father his truck keys?

What do you mean he is selling his truck, Mom?

Please don't tell me Mark's family got the ski boat!

Perfect.

(PAUSE; SLOWLY GROWING EXCITED)

Well, maybe Mark will ask *me* to go to the lake.

BEN'S MONOLOGUE

Cali Elizabeth Moore

I'm a guy. I know what it's like to meet a girl and think, "She is cute." I'm your average guy. But when you think that about my sister, it's a different story.

Sara is younger than me by eleven months, and ever since I can remember we have done everything together. We learned how to walk together and swim together. It's always been the two of us.

Here recently, however, boys have started to . . . *notice* Sara. I feel it's my place to take action at this point. I can't let just any old slime ball talk to my sister.

Unfortunately, I get no thanks, no kind words from my sister. She feels I am invading her "privacy" and "wrecking her social life" and "being a looser." And that is fine. She can think that now, but when she sees the guy who tried to get her number yesterday in twenty years and he's homeless, who do think she will thank? *Me*! ME, buddy!

So next time you see a girl that you think is cute and you just want to waltz on over and say hello, remember it could be Sara, my sister. And if it is, I'm there. You may not see me, but I am *there*!

So watch it, punk!

PLAY IT COOL

Regina Moore

Hey, Mom . . . I was wondering . . . could we stop and pick up Anna on the way to the mall? She's going shopping, too.

I mean, we're going to the mall at the same time. Which I guess means that we are going shopping together. Which doesn't mean we're going together as a couple. I know we are going to the mall together but I don't know if we are going . . . *out.*

(FRUSTRATED AND CONFUSED)

She never talks to me, but after the football game she asked me if I was going to the mall tomorrow—I mean today. So, I said I didn't know. I freaked out a little when she said, "Well, if you're going, can I get a ride?"

What does *that* mean? That she wants a ride to the mall or that she wants to go with me to the mall? How does she even know if I like going to the mall?

Mom, when we get there . . . play it cool. Let me do all the talking, okay?

Here's the house.

Honk the horn; she said to honk the horn.

Here she comes; play it cool . . .

(*PAUSE; TRYING TO COMPOSE HIMSELF*)

. . . like me.

THE CHRISTMAS TREE

Regina Moore

A couple of years ago, my dad and I set out to find the family Christmas tree. Now, when Dad says we are going to look for the Christmas tree, I put on extra socks, a pair of jeans, long underwear, two or three sweaters, gloves, and always a scarf.

My dad comes from a family that takes that job very serious. Grandpa, Dad, and his brothers would actually make it out to be a mission given by some English Royalty. You couldn't just pick the first tree you saw; no, no, no . . . it had to be the *perfect* tree. Exactly seven feet tall, each branch the perfect length, and it had to be freshly cut. He said it was less of a fire hazard and the smell . . . well, that was why the tree had to be real. Grandpa said, "If the tree is real, then Christmas is real." I didn't understand that way of thinking. I mean, a tree is a tree, right?

Well, my dad seemed to agree with my Grandpa, so off we went. It didn't matter that the weatherman was predicting a snow storm. It was our job; we were the men. We had to bring back the tree.

Mom packed us a bag of food. Dad had our sleeping bags. That should have told me what was in store for us. It was cold before it started getting dark. I told Dad we should start heading back, but no. He said we would find the tree in the morning. I couldn't feel my feet or my hands. I was ready to go home .

Just as the morning light came over the hills, I heard something. I mean, it was still dark and I didn't know what was out there. I don't know; something just made me go.

I walked to the top of the clearing and there it was. The morning sun was hitting it like it was lit up and just waiting for ornaments to be placed on its branches. It was the most beautiful Christmas tree I had ever seen. Well, I cut it down and brought it back; Dad agreed. Now Dad has passed down this important tradition to me.

I am sure that when I try to explain what an amazing experience it will be, my son will think the same thing I thought. It will only be when he finds the perfect Christmas tree that he will understand.

Words on a Page: Monologues for Young Performers

Part 4
Young Women & Young Men

Monologues are used to capture emotion, create atmosphere, and make the listener embrace their world. A strong monologue is an invaluable tool. But it's the responsibility of the actors performing the monologues to make us encounter the reality of the story. Their job is to make even the professional listener think, "Wait . . . this is a *monologue*, right?" When you audition, there are many actors going into the casting room delivering the same lines. If you want to be chosen for the part, give them something no one else will.

The monologues in this section are suitable for boys or girls. The actors' individual spin is what transforms the story, making the character become male or female. Remember to select your monologue carefully, reading through each option before making your decision. Choose a subject you can truly connect with, and then own it. You only have a short time to make your impression. Make each second count!

HORRIBLE PIANO PLAYER

Cali Elizabeth Moore

All kids have hobbies. Some sing. Some play basketball. Some collect stuffed animals. But no matter what the hobby is, the kid does it because it interests them. They do it because they enjoy it.

My hobby is playing the piano and I hate it. It does not interest me. I do not enjoy it. You may ask yourself, "Then why would you do it? Why would you play the piano if you don't like it?" The answer is simple: I don't have a choice.

Ever since I was five years old, my mother has had me in piano lessons. She thinks it will create character and help me to learn work ethic. I think she is nuts!

Every Wednesday at 5:00 P.M., my piano teacher, Mrs. Bradley, comes to my house. She makes me play the piece I was supposed to practice that week. She watches me with judging eyes. Mrs. Bradley is a very scary lady.

First off, Mrs. Bradley has to be at least 98 years old and I am being generous. Secondly, she has long bony skeleton fingers that drag across the keys. Third, she hums while I play. I know that doesn't sound like a big deal, but she hums louder than the grand piano sometimes. And let's just say she could use some tuning.

She always tells my mother I am making excellent progress and that I am a regular Mozart when the lesson is over. The truth is, I am horrible. I know I am. And my mom knows, too. And if Mrs. Bradley would listen to me play instead of humming the whole lesson, *she* would know I'm no good!

No one will admit it, though. Denial has swept the household.

Is there no one who will speak the truth?

Am I doomed to play the piano for the rest of my life?

New Kid at Lunch

Cali Elizabeth Moore

Have you ever had the feeling that you're going to be sick? You know, like the one where it comes from your gut and you just feel helpless? Well, that is how I felt today in the lunchroom.

Today was the first day of school. Now, I'm not a Kindergartener. I knew what the first day was going to be like. But I'm at a new school this year. So I don't know anyone.

My plan was simple. I was going to make as many friends as possible by lunch. I figured as long as I had someone to sit with at lunch, I'd be fine.

When I got to school, I found out lunch was at 11:30. I started talking to everyone I could in the class. But out of the corner of my eye, I was always watching the clock. And time went by fast—*too* fast.

By 11:15, all I knew was that Sarah was a cheerleader, John was bad at math, David had failed this grade last year, and I was going to be sitting alone. I was terrified. I could just picture myself sitting alone in the corner of the cafeteria as the tumble weeds bounced by.

I got to the cafeteria and got in the lunch line. I tried to talk to the girl in front of me, but I think she was a foreign exchange student. She just looked at me puzzled.

Finally, the moment came. I had paid for my lunch and was standing in front of the cafeteria just looking at the kids like I was a zombie or something. That feeling took over. I thought to myself, "This is it. I'm going to be forever known as the new kid that threw up in front of everyone on the first day of school."

And then, something amazing happened. A teacher walked up to me and said, "You must be new. During the first week of school, we have assigned seating in the cafeteria. Your seat is right over there."

I wanted to scream I was so excited! But then I would have been known as the kid who screamed for no reason in front of everyone on the first day of school. So I just walked to my seat and sat down.

As the sick feeling went away, I looked down at my tray: empty. I guess I must have been so nervous in the lunch line that I forgot to get food. Well, hunger is a small price to pay to look cool on the first day at a new school.

SUMMER CAMP

Regina Moore

I am packing to go to summer camp. I know it seems like I'm pretty young to be leaving for two whole weeks without my mom or my dad, but I think I am ready. I stay all night all the time with my friends. I go to Grandma's on summer break, too. Last time I stayed one full week at my grandma's and I didn't get home sick once. I used to get home sick and it was hard for me to stay even one night away, but not anymore.

(HESITATE)

I'm really doing this for my parents.

My mom was a little difficult to convince that I was ready for camp this year. She didn't like the idea that we would be staying in cabins out in the woods and that there would be a pond nearby. You know how parents are. They think you're a great swimmer until you're out of their sight.

My mom and dad are going to be visiting on the weekends; they insisted. I think they were afraid I would miss them. It is really going to be hard on Mom and

Dad when I leave home. I thought this could be good for them. Kind of prepare them for when I'll leave home forever.

Don't mention that to them right now. I don't think they could handle that.

BEING FAMOUS

Regina Moore

I wish we could just be a normal family. You know, go out to dinner at a regular restaurant or go to the movies. It is never normal, no matter what we do. We cannot go to the grocery store without a bodyguard. It would be so nice to go anywhere, anyplace, where no one stops us to ask for a picture or an autograph.

Most people are nice and understand they are asking my mom to take time from her family, to stop what she is doing to show them attention. But some people are not so nice.

One time we were in a private dining room in a restaurant because it was my sister's engagement party and a lady walked in to ask for an autograph. The door was shut, but she walked right in. It was so embarrassing for my mom. She tried to explain that it was a private party and that maybe at another time it would be okay. The lady got mad and said "that's what you should expect when you're famous." I got mad and I told that lady that I was tired of sharing her with inconsiderate people who never thought of what they were doing every time they interrupted our lives. The lady just looked at me and said, "How rude." I thought mom would agree, but she acted upset and ignored me the rest of the night.

I have to share her with millions of people every day. When she sings about her love for the important things in life, that is what makes her fans love her. She makes them feel special, like she is singing to them. That's why they love her.

Why don't I feel like her songs are about *me*, that she is singing to *me*, that she loves *me*?

VACATION

Regina Moore

When you're going on vacation you should get excited and think about how much fun you're going to have, but that is not the way it is around my house. First, my parents start arguing about where we are going and how much money we are going to spend. Then it happens: they start talking about the hotel.

My mom remembers the dreaded Florida trip at the Lagoona Hotel. The ad read, "Sandy beaches, beautiful rooms, and a delicious menu for the family." What hotel were *they* talking about? The Lagoona Hotel was at a dead end street with twenty feet of beach right next to a city dump. The hotel had a restaurant, if that is what you call it. They had one very mad waitress, a cook that looked like he had just escaped from prison and the food . . . terrible.

The worst part of the whole trip was the hotel room. My mom is very particular about hotel rooms and this place was right out of a horror movie. We walked into a dirty room and the bathroom was either leaking from the sink or the shower, which of course means bugs—BIG BUGS! And my mom does *not* like bugs.

When it was time to go to bed, Mom would not let us get under the sheets. She laid the towels on top of the comforter and that is the way we slept until we heard the police. The Lagoona Hotel was a very popular spot.

Yeah, Dad has to hear about the Lagoona Hotel every time we talk about a vacation. Dad said this year is going to be different and that Mom is going to love this trip.

I hope so, for his sake.

THE MOVE

Cali Elizabeth Moore

I love Williamsburg. We just moved here a month ago. It's great. Our house here is so much bigger. I don't have to share a bathroom with my sister. We have a pool now, too. Mom loves all the space.

I've made some new friends already. They're pretty cool. They live in my neighborhood. We all walk to school together sometimes.

(*PAUSE*)

It's just that sometimes, I miss Radnor. Radnor is where we use to live. I miss my best friend, Paul. We were next door neighbors. We used to do everything together. He said we'd always be friends even if I didn't live in Radnor. I know that's not true, though. I'm sure he's found a new best friend now.

I miss my old school, too. I knew all the teachers. Even the ones I didn't like, I think I kind of miss. I wish I could just stand in my old house one more time. I'd just like to lie on the carpet in front of the fire place, or slide down the banister, or run out of the back door in the kitchen and hear the screen door slam . . . just one more time.

I guess things are different here and I need to deal with that. I should be excited that I get to live in a new house and make new friends. It's just that deep down, no matter how hard I try to be excited, I'm not.

BAD GRADE

Cali Elizabeth Moore

An *F*! I got an *F*! This can't be right, Mrs. Harold! I studied ALL week for this test. I stayed up until 11:30 every night. I made note cards and joined a study group and everything.

Are you *sure* this grade is right? I mean, I saw Thomas's grade he got a B-. That *can't* be right. We all know he's not the brightest crayon in the box. He made an F on a spelling test and there were only three words on the entire test! *Three words!*

Or what about Meredith? I know she's not as smart as I am, but she made a C. We always make close to the same grade. (POINTING TO THE PAPER) This just *can't* be right!

(PAUSING TO GAIN COMPOSURE)

Okay. Maybe we started out on the wrong foot. I apologize. I'm sure we can come to some kind of understanding. How do you feel about retakes? Like, what if I was to skip lunch, come here, and take the test over right in front of you? Or if that isn't a good time for you I could take it right now. Just give me the test!

(TEACHER SHAKES HER HEAD "NO")

Okay! You know what? FINE! I guess I should just accept it. I got an F. But can you accept that you will be the cause of my failure to attend college? Or to get a job when I'm older? Or the failure to support my family when I'm married with children with mouths to feed? I might as well be homeless, thanks to you! So I hope you can sleep at night!

GRANDMA

Regina Moore

Grandma called my mom today to say she does not want to live in the retirement home anymore. Her closest friend Sophie passed away two months ago and Grandma has not smiled once since then. Sophie and Grandma were always playing cards, watching television shows, or just sitting together listening to music. They were always together. She must be very lonely. I have a best friend named Taylor and we play cards, watch television, and listen to music, too. I'd be sad if my best friend was gone.

Hey, I think Mom should ask Grandma to come live here. We could take care of her the way she took care of us. She raised Mom and babysat me while Mom was at work. Grandma should come live with us because family should take care of family. Grandma taught us that family is one of the most important things in life. We could play cards, but I don't think she would want to watch my television shows or listen to my music. I know—Grandma is a *great* cook. She can teach me how to cook. I like art and Grandma loves to draw. There are *lots* of things we can do together.

(*HEARING THE DOORBELL RING*)

Is that somebody at the door? I'll get it, Mom!

Grandma, I didn't know that you were coming to visit.

You're staying?

I'm so glad you are here.

You can sleep in my room.

I'll get your suitcase.

CHORES

Regina Moore

I asked my mom for a weekly allowance and she said I would have to do chores. *Chores?* What are we living in, the 18ᵀᴴ century? She said I would have to work it off. *Work it off?* Can't she just give me the money?

I couldn't believe the list Mom put on the refrigerator: wash dishes (I've done *that* before), dust the furniture, pickup my bedroom, make my bed, take my dirty clothes to the laundry room *and* wash them *and* help put the laundry away.

Am I a maid? She wants me to do that *every day*. I can *not* spend all my time cleaning. I won't have time to go out with my friends. But if I don't do the chores, I won't have money to spend when I go out with my friends.

She's got me. It looks like I don't have a choice. There's a big party for Chelsea coming up, so I have to have cash. If I do my homework at school and come straight home, I think I can get it all finished before the party.

You know, it is amazing if you organize your time.

You have time to do it all.

(HESITATE; YOU'RE THINKING)

You think Mom was thinking the same thing?

WHAT COULD HAVE BEEN

Cali Elizabeth Moore

When I was six years old, I was in a bad car accident. It was a long time ago and I'm okay now. It's just that I think about it a lot.

My mom was driving me to my friend's birthday party. I was really excited because Mom let me wear my cape. I felt like a superhero. We were stopped at a stoplight. The light turned green. I said, "Green means go, Mom." And then everything after that is in slow motion.

I saw another woman driving toward us. My mom threw her arm in front of me. She slammed on the brakes. I heard the cars crash together. I'll never forget that sound. I heard glass shattering and my mom screamed my name. Then everything turned over. Our car landed on its side. There was a lot of smoke. I yelled for mom, but she didn't yell back. I was bleeding and I was really scared.

I started crawling over to my mom's side of the car. She was lying there with her eyes closed. She was bleeding, too. I started crying and screaming for help.

A few minutes later, the police came. They took my mom and me away in an ambulance. The lady who hit us was taken away in a helicopter. I'd never seen one before. It all felt like it wasn't real.

Later we found out that the lady who hit us was a drunk driver. Imagine being drunk at 2:00 in the afternoon and then wanting to drive. Then I was too young to understand, but as I've gotten older . . . it just makes me so mad. The lady died that day. She could have lived a full life. She might have had kids or a husband or . . . I don't know. I just can't believe all that is gone because she chose to drive drunk.

And what about my mom and me? We could have died! We could have been gone just like *that* because of a stupid choice some lady we didn't even know made. There are so many great things that have happened to me since then that might have never happen if . . . if things had turned out different. You know?

Luckily, my mom and I were fine. But every once in a while, I think about that afternoon. I think about what happened that day . . . and what could have happened.

ICE CREAM

Regina Moore

All the ice cream I can eat. That's what Mom said. She said I could eat as much ice cream as I wanted. That is how they get you to agree; to get you to go to the doctor; to get you to go to the hospital without a fight.

All of that changes when they take away your clothes and make you get into a thin gown that ties in the back. That's so they can sneak up on you and give you a shot where you do *not* want to get one.

She said it wouldn't hurt. Well, the shots hurt, and when I woke up my throat hurt.

Mom said if I had had my tonsils out when I was younger, then it wouldn't hurt at all. Why didn't she do it? Why didn't she have my tonsils out when I wouldn't notice? She's my mom. She should take care of things. I told her that. But she said I didn't *need* to have them taken out. Why don't they just take them out when you're born? It would make it easier on all of us.

Well, at least I get to lie in bed and watch TV with a constant flow of ice cream being placed in front of me. I have tried every flavor. I think plain chocolate is still my favorite. I guess it isn't *that* bad. If eating ice cream is the only medicine I have to take until I feel better, well then *(PUTTING ON BEST SAD FACE)*, I feel awful!

Having Fun

Regina Moore

The other day, my parents surprised us and said they were taking us to the circus. At first, I didn't want to go, but Dad said he wanted me to put down the video games and take a break from TV to have some real fun. Mom said I didn't know what fun was until I had been to the circus. I just didn't want to go. How lame, right?

Well, I went and I saw some cool things like lions and their trainers. Oh, and there was the lady hanging from a really high rope; she just let go. It was *crazy*.

(GETTING EXCITED)

Dad bought us some hotdogs, popcorn, and cotton candy. And then there were a whole lot of people dressed up like clowns running around chasing each other. Some were on tall bikes, riding around, but the funniest part was when . . . I don't even *know* how many of them got into a tiny car.

(STARTING TO LAUGH) I mean, this car was *really* small and the clowns started pilling in. They were hanging out the windows, and the sunroof. It made us all laugh.

It was fun.

All the way home we talked about what we saw, and after dinner, too. We laughed about everything. You know, Mom and Dad were right. We really had fun. I hope we do it again soon.

Holiday Shame

Cali Elizabeth Moore

I can't stand being a kid around holidays. I mean, my parents always try to build it up, but no matter what holiday it is, it's always a gigantic let down! New Year's, Easter, 4ᵀᴴ of July, Halloween, Thanksgiving, Christmas . . . they are complete wastes of time and ultimately cause me shame.

Okay, so you're probably thinking that Christmas has got to be great. Everyone loves presents and Santa and candy canes. Well, that's not how it is for me. First of all, I am allergic to candy canes. They make me break out in hives. As for Santa, please. The veil was lifted from that mystery years ago. And then there are the presents. My parents believe that "it is better to give than to receive." So every year I have to give my presents away to the less fortunate. *(PAUSE)* I'm not kidding.

Halloween is no better. I'm not allowed to dress up like normal things because my grandmother makes my costumes and she picks them out. Like last year; I was a daffodil because that's her favorite flower.

I think the worst is Easter. My mother makes me participate in the Easter play. Every year I'm some kid that Jesus heals. And every year you can hear my mother sobbing as I am being healed. Her cries can be heard all around the sanctuary. It's so embarrassing. Then, we go to my grandmother's house and we have an Easter egg hunt. But when it's over, I have to give all the eggs and candy to the cousin who has the least eggs and candy— because my parents think "it's better to give than to receive." Since this happens every year, my cousins don't even try anymore. It's horrible!

When I'm older, I won't do this to my kids. I'll let them play with fireworks, because I've never met a kid who burned their hand off playing with them. And on New Year's, I'll let my kids stay up and watch the ball drop. And in my house, it will be better to receive than give.

BURGER

Cali Elizabeth Moore

A few years ago, our family got a dog named Burger. We called him that because he loved burgers. Even when we made them at home, he licked his lips and wagged his tail.

Burger was different from other dogs. He could do lots of tricks. He could catch a frisbee and play dead. Sometimes he would stand up on his hind legs like a person if you held a treat up. He was a serious dog, too. He wouldn't let strangers get too close to me or my brother. He would bark and howl if someone he didn't know came in the house. Mom said Burger was our watch dog. I guess he was just trying to protect us.

One night, my brother and I were at home with a babysitter when a man tried to break in. He got in the door and Burger jumped up on him and started barking and biting him. We ran into the kitchen and called the police.

Burger was still biting him. The man pushed Burger off and he started kicking Burger. By then, we could hear the sirens from the police cars. The man ran away.

I ran to Burger. He was whining but he wasn't moving. There was blood in his fur. The babysitter tried to pull me off of him, but I told her that I wanted to be with Burger.

Then Burger closed his eyes.

They didn't open again.

I'll never forget that day. But I'll never forget Burger. He was the bravest dog in the whole world.

THE ONLY KID

Regina Moore

Too bad things aren't like they used to be. I mean, when I was the only kid in the family, it was important to Mom and Dad that I had everything I wanted. Now when I want to go somewhere or buy something, my little brother has to be considered. Everything has to be fair; even. We both have to get the same things, but I am older. Doesn't that count for something?

Sometimes there is just no way that he can do or have the things I should. He is too little to go to the basketball games. If he does go, he's a brat the whole time. When I want to go to the mall with friends, they say I can't go unless he goes along. I can't wait to grow up, so I won't have a shadow anymore.

REGINA MOORE

Regina Moore has been in the entertainment industry for over 30 years. First an actress, Regina is now a casting director in the areas of film, television, commercials, print, music videos, and live performance. As an instructor, she is known for her ability to recognize potential and encouraging the growing actor with her straight forward, no nonsense approach. Her workshops deal with the audition process and improv. Regina relates to the actor regardless of whether they are a beginner or a professional. She is accomplished in the field of casting and is also a creative voice for project development. She is also a casting consultant working in relationship to television hosts, actors, live performers, and audience-related programming.

CALI ELIZABETH MOORE

Cali Elizabeth Moore has acted in film, television, commercials, and theatre for most of her life. Her first acting job was at two years old. The experience of being a child actor is what prompted her to co-author this book. In addition to her acting, Cali has been an acting coach and teacher for nearly a decade, working from the west to east coast. Cali currently lives in New York with her husband Matt, where she is pursuing her career.

ENDORSEMENTS FOR
YOUNG PERFORMERS' SUMMER ACTING CAMP

"Bryce's first audition was with Regina. We learned quickly how important it is to get the right training. Regina and Cali Moore really know how to communicate with kids. The classes and materials they provided helped my daughter become the actress she is today. After their training, Bryce went on to book national commercials and work in film and television."

Courtney Hitchcock, mother of Bryce Hitchcock

You may know Bryce from such parts as the lead role in "Solution Street" (the new Disney. com / Disney 365 / Disney Channel show); "My Name is Earl" (20th Century Fox television show), "Lie to Me" (20th Century Fox television show), Veggie Tales' "Saint Nicholas: A Story of Joyful Giving" (vocal talent for animated feature film), and State Farm's Embrace Life television commercial.

"I highly recommend Moore Casting's acting workshops. Regina and Cali really prepared my boys for the audition process, especially learning how to effectively deliver monologues in a way that captures attention. They helped my sons not only book projects but gave them the tools to bring out the best in themselves while auditioning and on set. Now they are consistently able to take those skills and put them to good use in the Atlanta and LA markets."

Ann Rousseau Morris, mother of Luke and Seth Morris

You may know Luke from such parts as "All the King's Men" (Columbia Pictures feature film); "Claire" (Hallmark made-for-television movie), "Warm Springs" (HBO made-for-television movie), and national television commercials for JC Penney and Chevrolet. You may know Seth from such parts as a co-star role in "Big Love" (HBO television show), "Warm Springs" (HBO made-for-television movie), and national television commercials for KFC and Gamewave.

"We rave about their classes and workshops! Regina and her staff are knowledgeable and give first-hand advice and instruction from a Casting Director's point of view. I highly recommend Moore Casting!"

Joy Pervis
Talent Agent, J Pervis Talent Agency
National Talent Scout, Osbrink Agency

Young Performers' Summer Acting Camp

7 to 17 year olds: Full Day
Monday — Friday; 9:00am to 5:00pm

4 to 6 year olds: Half Day
Monday — Friday; 9:00am to 12:00 noon

developed for the serious actor

At the request of Talent Agencies, Casting Director Regina Moore has developed a remarkable week of training specifically focused on the areas in which children are asked to perform as professional actors.

"As a Casting Director, I see children with enormous amounts of potential, yet there's little training available that's focused enough to discover and develop it," Regina says. "I wanted to focus on what work is available to children in this market, so I created a dedicated week of training for children focusing on commercials, monologues, theatre, film, television, script-critique, auditioning, improvisational acting, voice-over technique, and more. The camp is a lot of fun, but it was created for the serious child actor who is interested in pursuing an acting career."

This fun and intense acting camp is conducted one week during the months of June, July, and August. The same curriculum is taught each month, but offered three times each year for your convenience.

Visit our website for dates, prices, and registration information:
www.moorecasting.com